Angels We Have Heard

*Christmas Eve Candlelight
And Communion Service*

Mary Lu Warstler

CSS Publishing Company, Inc., Lima, Ohio

ANGELS WE HAVE HEARD

For more information about CSS Publishing Company resources, visit our website at
www.csspub.com.

ISBN 0-7880-1837-X   PRINTED IN U.S.A.

To my husband Rodney, who by his steadfast love has made it possible for me to spend time writing.

Introduction

Christmas Eve is a special time in any church. Since I have been in ministry, I have had communion with the service each year. It was what the people wanted and I found it to be spiritually uplifting. After all, Christmas would mean nothing without the death and resurrection. However, this service is written in such a way that the Communion Service could be omitted and it would still be a complete worship experience. (If you do not want the communion service, omit material from the Hymn: "Cross Of Jesus, Cross Of Sorrow" through the Prayer After Communion. Begin again with the carol: "Angels We Have Heard on High.") If you are not using a choir, the congregation may sing the Introit.

Many of the favorite carols are included. People never seem to tire of hearing and singing the carols of Christmas. Angels are also a vital part of the Christmas story — from the promise to Abraham to the fulfillment of that promise in Bethlehem. The scriptures are all paraphrased to enable dialogue between angels and human-kind. Portions are represented from Genesis, Matthew, and Luke.

While I have included several speaking parts — angels, shepherds, narrator — it is also easy to combine parts and use one angel and one shepherd. When I first used this service only the liturgist and I were the speakers. It is not necessary to have costumes, but if you want them, keep it simple: white robes for angels, simple robes for others.

Everyone — well, almost everyone — loves candlelight for Christmas Eve. But for safety's sake, please be very cautious, especially when small children are present. Hold the lit candle upright at all times. Dip only the unlit candle. Extinguish the candles as soon as the hymn is sung.

Please do not try to leave or move about while carrying a lit candle!

God has blessed me with the ability to write a service like this and an enjoyment in doing so. I pray that you, the reader, will also receive a blessing when you use all or part of it.

Worship Bulletin

Angels We Have Heard

Christmas Eve Candlelight And Communion Service

Prelude

Service Of Acolytes

Introit   (Tune "Silent Night")   Choir
Fear ye not, Fear ye not; Behold I bring good tidings to you,
Peace on earth now let us sing, Peace on earth now let us sing,
Glory to God in the Highest, Glory to God on High.

Call To Worship   Responsively
Liturgist: "Fear not, for behold I bring you good tidings of great
          joy."
People: What news do you bring?
Liturgist: "Unto you is born this day a Savior who is Christ the
          Lord."
People: He brings joy to the world and peace on earth.

Prayer   In Unison
**O God, who makes us glad with the yearly remembrance of
the birth of your only Son, Jesus, grant that we may joyfully
receive him as our Savior and Redeemer that we may have
peace on earth. Amen.**

Hymn   "Angels From The Realms Of Glory"

Welcome

Passing Of The Peace

Announcements

Call To Stewardship   Liturgist

Offertory

Giving Of Our Christmas Gifts

Doxology   In Unison

Prayer Of Dedication   Liturgist

The Message In Word And Song

Carol   "O Word Of God Incarnate" (v. 1)

Dialogue: Angels and Abraham   Genesis 18:2-3, 9-10

Of the Father's Love Begotten 184

Carol   ~~"Watchman, Tell Us Of The Night" (v. 1)~~

Dialogue: Angel and Zechariah   Luke 1:5-25

Carol   "To A Maid Engaged To Joseph" (v. 1)

Dialogue: Angel and Mary   Luke 1:26-38

Anthem

~~**Carol**   "O Little Town Of Bethlehem" (v. 1)~~

Dialogue: Angel and Joseph   Matthew 1:18-25

Anthem

Anthem   ~~"Born 'Neath A Star"~~   ~~Choir~~

Carol   "The First Noel" (v. 1)

Dialogue: Angel and Shepherds   Luke 2:8-14

~~**Carol**~~   *anthem*   ~~"Away In A Manger" (v. 1)~~

Dialogue: Angel and Stable Boy

[handwritten: Lo, How A Rose E'er Blooming]

Hymn   "Cross Of Jesus, Cross Of Sorrow" (v. 1)

Service Of Holy Communion
  Words of Consecration   Pastor
  Prayer   Pastor
  Serving of Bread and Cup
  Prayer after Communion   In Unison
  **We give you thanks, most gracious God, for allowing us to
  share in this feast as your family and to be fed with the
  bread of heaven. Give us grace that we all may grow in
  love, glorifying you in all things. Through Jesus Christ our
  Lord. Amen.**

Carol   "Angels We Have Heard On High" (v. 1)

Dialogue: Angel and "Modern Person"

Carol   "Silent Night" (vv. 1 and 2)

Lighting Of Candles
(*For safety's sake, please dip only unlit candle. Help children with
candles, and please extinguish candles before leaving at the end
of the hymn.*)

Benediction   Pastor

Postlude

Complete Service And Dialogues

₫ngels We Have Heard

*Christmas Eve Candlelight
And Communion Service*

Prelude

Service Of Acolytes

Introit   (Tune "Silent Night")   Choir or Congregation
Fear ye not, Fear ye not; Behold I bring good tidings to you.
Peace on earth now let us sing, Peace on earth now let us sing,
Glory to God in the Highest, Glory to God on High.

Call To Worship   Responsively
Liturgist: "Fear not, for behold I bring you good tidings of great
             joy."
People: What news do you bring?
Liturgist: "Unto you is born this day a Savior who is Christ the
             Lord."
People: He brings joy to the world and peace on earth.

Prayer   In Unison
O God, who makes us glad with the yearly remembrance of the
birth of your only Son, Jesus, grant that we may joyfully receive
him as our Savior and Redeemer that we may have peace on earth.
Amen.

Hymn   "Angels From The Realms Of Glory"

Welcome

Passing Of The Peace

11

Call To Stewardship   Liturgist

On this night when we celebrate the gift of God's own Son, let us bring our gifts and offerings in honor and love of that Gift.

Offertory

Giving Of Our Christmas Gifts

Doxology   In Unison

Prayer Of Dedication   Liturgist

We bring our tithes and gifts unto you, O God, as we celebrate the remembrance of your birth. Accept them — gift and giver — for your use. Amen.

The Message In Word And Song
Carol   "O Word Of God Incarnate" (v. 1)

Dialogue: Angels and Abraham[1]
(*Three Angels and Abraham enter*)

Narrator: Angels have been messengers of God since the beginning of time. They have visited earth to give news, announce joy, warn people, and simply be a go-between for God and his earthly creation.

Angel 1: Look, there is Abraham by the oaks of Mamre. He is sitting by his tent in the shade. The heat seems to bother humans. He has seen us.

Angel 2: Is it safe?

Angel 3: What do we say?

Angel 1: Let me handle it. He is running to meet us. Come, we will just visit as God instructed us to do.

Abraham: Welcome, travelers. Come, sit and rest awhile. I will bring cool water for your feet. After you rest, I will bring food for you to eat that you may not faint on your journey.

Angel 1: Thank you, sir. We will do as you have said.

Abraham: Sarah, quickly make some cakes. Servants, quickly prepare a feast. We have company. We must not let them go away hungry. (*Pauses*) Here, the food is ready. Eat and drink to your fill.

Angel 1: It is very good of you to care for our needs.

Angel 2: Where is Sarah, your wife?

Abraham: She is in the tent.

Angel 1: I will return this way in the spring. When I return, Sarah will have a son.

Angel 3: Oh, Sarah laughs, does she?

Angel 2: Does she think she is too old?

Angel 1: With God all things are possible.

Carol   "Watchman, Tell Us Of The Night" (v. 1)

Dialogue: Angel and Zechariah[2]

Narrator: When Herod was king of Judea, a priest named Zechariah was serving in the temple. A whole multitude of people were praying outside at the hour of incense. Zechariah should have been alone, but he was not.

13

Angel: There is Zechariah in the temple, faithfully performing his duties. He thinks this is just another day like all other days. He is going to be surprised. Hail, Zechariah! The Lord is with you.

Zechariah: Who are you? How did you get past the temple guards? But wait ... you are different. You are not human.

Angel: Do not be afraid, Zechariah. I have come to bring you good news. Your prayers have been heard. Your wife, Elizabeth, will bear you a son. You will call his name, John.

Zechariah: Surely you realize that I am old. Elizabeth also has passed the age of bearing children. We stopped praying for a son long ago. It is impossible.

Angel: Nothing is impossible with our God. She will bear a son. You will have joy and gladness. Many will rejoice with you. He will be great before the Lord. You must keep him from strong drink for the Holy Spirit will be with him from birth. He will lead many to God in the Spirit of Elijah. He will prepare the people for the Lord — the Messiah.

Zechariah: This is wonderful, but how shall I know? As I said, I am old and Elizabeth is advanced in years as well.

Angel: I am Gabriel. I stand in for the presence of God. I was sent to speak to you and bring you good news. Behold, you will be in silence — not hearing or speaking until this thing comes to pass. Go now. The people wait for you.

Zechariah: (*Pauses*) It has been a year since that strange day in the temple. Gabriel was right. We have our son. People thought we were strange when we named him John. That name is not in either of our families. Elizabeth is overjoyed. I can again hear and speak. But I am glad we are old. I do not believe we would want to live to see what is ahead for our son and his cousin, who is to be born to Mary.

Carol   "To A Maid Engaged To Joseph"[3] (v. 1)

Dialogue: Angel and Mary[4]

Narrator: Six months after the visit to Zechariah, the angel made another trip to earth, this time to a town in Galilee named Nazareth.

Angel: There is Mary. She is a young virgin who is betrothed to Joseph, the carpenter of Nazareth. Hail, Mary, O favored one! The Lord is with you.

Mary: What sort of greeting is this? Who are you? Why have you come to trouble me like this?

Angel: Do not be afraid, Mary. You have found favor with God. You have been chosen to bear God's Son. You will name him Jesus. He will be great. He will be called the Son of the Most High. God will give him the throne of David. He will reign over the house of Jacob forever. There will be no end to his kingdom.

Mary: How can this be? I am not even married yet.

Angel: The Holy Spirit will come upon you. The power of the Most High will overshadow you. Therefore, the child to be born will be called Holy — the Son of God. And, oh, by the way, your cousin Elizabeth, who is advanced in years, is in her sixth month. You see, with God nothing is impossible.

Mary: Behold, I am the Lord's servant. Let it be to me as you have said. I am willing.

Carol   "O Little Town Of Bethlehem" (v. 1)

Dialogue: Angel and Joseph[5]

Narrator: Joseph was a just man and he did not want to put Mary to shame. He had resolved to divorce her quietly. But God sent his messenger in a dream.

15

Joseph: What will people think? I cannot let them think that I had anything to do with this. And yet, I cannot believe that Mary would be unfaithful to me. She has always been so close to God — so close that I can almost believe her when she tells me it is God's Son she is carrying. But who ever heard of such a thing? It is impossible. I will simply divorce her quietly. I don't want to make a public example of her. But I must sleep on it. I will act tomorrow.

Angel: Joseph! Joseph, do not be afraid to take Mary as your wife. She has not been unfaithful to you. She has been chosen to be the mother of God's own Son. That which is conceived in her is of the Holy Spirit. She will have a son. You will call him Jesus. He will save his people from their sins.

Joseph: That was a strange dream. I wonder if it was a dream. Maybe ... maybe God was speaking to me. Yes, I believe it was the angel Mary told me about. I will trust God and take Mary as my wife. We will wait until after she gives birth to consummate our marriage. But now, we must get ready to go to Bethlehem to pay our tribute to Caesar.

Angel: Yes, Joseph will go to Bethlehem. Little does he know the kind of place in which they will spend the night when the child is born.

Anthem   "Born 'Neath A Star"   Choir
(or any other appropriate anthem or carol)

Carol   "The First Noel" (v. 1)

Dialogue: Angel and Shepherds[6]

Narrator: Mary and Joseph had traveled from Nazareth to Bethlehem to be enrolled and pay their taxes. They had no sooner arrived when Mary felt the first pangs of the approaching birth. Because there were so many people in Bethlehem to pay their taxes, there was no room to be had anywhere. A stable became their room for the night and a manger was the newborn baby's first cradle.

16

But surely the birth of the Son of God — the Prince of Peace — should be announced to *someone*!

Angel: It is time! I must announce the news to the world. But what is this? The crowds are not gathered as I had hoped they would be. I see only a few shepherds watching their sheep.

Shepherd 1: What is that light?

Shepherd 2: Who is singing in the night?

Angel: Do not be afraid, shepherds. I am bringing you good news of great joy which will come to all people. Tonight in Bethlehem, the City of David, a child is born, a Savior who is Christ the Lord. Go to Bethlehem and see him. You will find him wrapped in soft cloths, lying in a manger.

Shepherd 2: Listen. There are more angels singing.

Shepherd 1: Come, let us hurry to Bethlehem and see this thing which has happened.

Shepherd 2: A baby in a manger? A Savior?

Shepherd 1: Come, let us go and bow down before him.

Carol   "Away In A Manger" (v. 1)

Dialogue: Angel and Stable Boy

Angel: See the sad little stable boy in the far corner. He can neither speak nor hear. He had been sent to care for the needs of the animals. He made a clean bed of hay for the weary travelers and shared his meager supper with them. Now he is taking care of the little donkey so Joseph may stay close to Mary as she gives birth to the Son of God. The boy neither hears, nor speaks, but he knows what is to come.

Hymn   "Cross Of Jesus, Cross Of Sorrow" (v. 1)

Service Of Holy Communion

Words of Consecration   Pastor

The gift of God's Son did not end in that stable bare. That was only the beginning. The child grew to adulthood. He taught, healed, loved, and celebrated life. Before he left this earth, he gave us a symbol of remembrance and celebration.

On the night when he was betrayed, he took bread from the evening Passover meal. He broke it, as he had broken it so many times before, but this time was different. He said to his friends, "This bread is like my body which will be broken for you. As you eat it, remember, and give thanks to your God."

And then he took his cup, which was still full, and said to his friends, "Take this cup and share it. The red wine is like my blood which will flow for you. All of you drink from it and remember my words and be glad in your hearts."

Prayer   Pastor

Lord God, Father of our Lord Jesus Christ, even as Jesus blessed the bread and the wine on that night many centuries ago, we ask you to bless this bread and wine before us this Christmas Eve, 20___. May they be for us the body and blood of our Lord as we remember his birth and death and resurrection. In the Name of him, who was born this night, Jesus our Christ. Amen.

Serving of Bread and Cup

Prayer after Communion   In Unison

We give you thanks, most gracious God, for allowing us to share in this feast as your family and to be fed with the bread of heaven. Give us grace that we all may grow in love, glorifying you in all things. Through Jesus Christ our   Lord. Amen.

Carol   "Angels We Have Heard On High" (v. 1)

Dialogue: Angel and "Modern Person"

Angel: Things seem different in 20__. I cannot seem to speak with people today. Even when I say, "Fear not!" they don't seem to hear me. Can it be that they are not afraid of angels anymore?

Person: Many do not believe in angels. Many do not even believe in God's Son. But we who love him seek always to follow his ways and remember his birth. The outer noises of shoppers and traffic and the internal noises of stress and fear make us deaf to your soft, soothing voice.

Angel: But you remember the night the child was born even though you were not there. You remember the journey to Bethlehem, the stable, the shepherds — and even the angels. How can you remember what you have not seen?

Person: Because it is written in God's Book. It is taught from the time we are small. But most of all because Jesus lives within our hearts. We celebrate the anniversary of his birth each year with songs and prayers and candlelight. He is the Light of the World. Will you join me in giving the people the Light of the World?

(The two readers take their candles and light them from the altar candles. Ushers light their candles from the readers' candles. People in pews light theirs from the ushers' candles. Begin singing the carol while candles are being lit. Extinguish all other lights.)

Carol   "Silent Night" (vv. 1 and 2)

Lighting Of Candles

(For safety's sake, please dip only the unlit candle. Help children with candles, and please extinguish the candles before leaving at the end of the hymn.)

Benediction   Pastor
May you go in the peace of Christmas, given by the Father of Love
through the power of the Holy Spirit. May God's Light shine upon
you through this holy time. Amen.

Postlude

---

1. Genesis 18:2-3, 9-10

2. Luke 1:5-25

3. Found in *The United Methodist Hymnal*, p. 215.

4. Luke 1:26-38

5. Matthew 1:18-25

6. Luke 2:8-14